Happy Holidays!

HAPPY NEW YEAR!

By Alex Appleby

Gareth Stevens
Publishing

Please visit our website, www.garethstevens.com. For a free color catalog of all our high-quality books, call toll free 1-800-542-2595 or fax 1-877-542-2596.

Library of Congress Cataloging-in-Publication Data

Appleby, Alex.
Happy New Year! / by Alex Appleby.
   p. cm. — (Happy holidays!)
Includes index.
ISBN 978-1-4339-9945-1 (pbk.)
ISBN 978-1-4339-9946-8 (6-pack)
ISBN 978-1-4339-9943-7 (library binding)
1. New Year — Juvenile literature. I. Appleby, Alex. II. Title.
GT4905.A66 2014
394.2614—d23

First Edition

Published in 2014 by
Gareth Stevens Publishing
111 East 14th Street, Suite 349
New York, NY 10003

Copyright © 2014 Gareth Stevens Publishing

Editor: Ryan Nagelhout
Designer: Sarah Liddell

Photo credits: Cover, p. 1 (confetti) lupulluss/Shutterstock.com; cover, p. 1 (hats) Mike Flippo/Shutterstock.com; p. 5 © iStockphoto.com/katemoss2007; p. 7 iStock/Thinkstock.com; p. 9 © iStockphoto.com/ktaylorg; p. 11 Brand New Images/Stone/Getty Images; p. 13 Stockbyte/Thinkstock.com; p. 15 iStock/Thinkstock.com; pp. 17, 24 (ball) Mario Tama/Staff/Getty Images News/Getty Images; pp. 19, 24 (party) Purestock/ Thinkstock.com; p. 21 gosphotodesign/Shutterstock.com; p. 23 Alexandra Grablewski/The Image Bank/ Getty Images.

Printed in the United States of America

CPSIA compliance information: Batch #CW14GS: For further information contact Gareth Stevens, New York, New York at 1-800-542-2595.

Contents

New Year's is
a great holiday.

5

It happens over
two days!

It starts on the last day of the year.

It is also called
New Year's Eve.

"Eve" means
"the day before."

13

People stay up
very late.

Some people watch the ball drop.

Others go
to big parties.

19

People want
to have fun!

January 1 starts
a new year.
It is New Year's Day!

Words to Know

ball

party

Index